William James McPherson, Jr.

83

New Poetry from Knopf

JOHN LOGAN
Spring of the Thief: Poems 1960–1962

SYLVIA PLATH
The Colossus and Other Poems

W. D. SNODGRASS
Heart's Needle

ROBERT HILLYER
Collected Poems

WITTER BYNNER
New Poems 1960

CAVAFY, SIKELIANOS, SEFERIS,
ANTONIOU, ELYTIS, GATSOS
Six Poets of Modern Greece
Edited and Translated by Edmund Keeley
and Philip Sherrard

These are BORZOI BOOKS
published by ALFRED A. KNOPF, *New York*

SELECTED POEMS

SELECTED
POEMS

John Crowe Ransom

A REVISED AND ENLARGED EDITION

New York · Alfred · A · Knopf

1963

Preface

THIS EDITION of *Selected Poems* contains all that were in the original edition. Some of them have been gone over critically and revised a little; but perhaps the new phrases will not perceptibly be out of tone with the body of them that is left untouched. One poem's title has been changed; from "Tom, Tom, the Piper's Son" to "The Vanity of the Bright Young Men." But in addition to the original poems I have entered, at the places where they seem to belong chronologically, a few others taken from my old single volumes. I shall not name them here, because the test of their belonging in the selection is whether the reader will want to stop and raise the question in his own right when he happens to come upon them. The total volume of my verse is not very large, and the *Selected Poems* will have to be modest proportionately.

But the greatest pleasure in preparing this edition came from the last two items of the text. "Master's in the

Garden Again" is a completely new version of the old and rather ignominious "Conrad in Twilight," elaborating it as the situation demanded in a style which did not try to resemble that of the original, except partly in the second of the three movements. This is the first verse I have written in more than twenty years, and it was very hard trying to "get my hand in" again. I do not know how well I succeeded.

The last item is "Prelude to an Evening: Revised and Explicated." The original eight stanzas remain pretty much what they were, but five new stanzas have been added which change the ending completely. The prose commentary follows the poem. Both this item and the preceding one have been published in the *Kenyon Review*.

JOHN CROWE RANSOM

Gambier, Ohio

Contents

SELECTED POEMS

Winter Remembered

Two evils, monstrous either one apart,
Possessed me, and were long and loath at going:
A cry of Absence, Absence, in the heart,
And in the wood the furious winter blowing.

Think not, when fire was bright upon my bricks,
And past the tight boards hardly a wind could enter,
I glowed like them, the simple burning sticks,
Far from my cause, my proper heat and center.

Better to walk forth in the frozen air
And wash my wound in the snows; that would be healing;
Because my heart would throb less painful there,
Being caked with cold, and past the smart of feeling.

And where I walked, the murderous winter blast
Would have this body bowed, these eyeballs streaming,
And though I think this heart's blood froze not fast
It ran too small to spare one drop for dreaming.

Dear love, these fingers that had known your touch,
And tied our separate forces first together,
Were ten poor idiot fingers not worth much,
Ten frozen parsnips hanging in the weather.

Miriam Tazewell

When Miriam Tazewell heard the tempest bursting
And his wrathy whips across the sky drawn crackling
She stuffed her ears for fright like a young thing
And with heart full of the flowers took to weeping.

But the earth shook dry his old back in good season,
He had weathered storms that drenched him deep as
       this one,
And the sun, Miriam, ascended to his dominion,
The storm was withered against his empyrean.

After the storm she went forth with skirts kilted
To see in the strong sun her lawn deflowered,
Her tulip, iris, peony strung and pelted,
Pots of geranium spilled and the stalks naked.

The spring transpired in that year with no flowers
But the regular stars went busily on their courses,
Suppers and cards were calendared, and some bridals,
And the birds demurely sang in the bitten poplars.

To Miriam Tazewell the whole world was villain
To prosper when the fragile babes were fallen,
And not to unstop her own storm and be maudlin,
For weeks she went untidy, she went sullen.

4

Dead Boy

The little cousin is dead, by foul subtraction,
A green bough from Virginia's aged tree,
And none of the county kin like the transaction,
Nor some of the world of outer dark, like me.

A boy not beautiful, nor good, nor clever,
A black cloud full of storms too hot for keeping,
A sword beneath his mother's heart—yet never
Woman bewept her babe as this is weeping.

A pig with a pasty face, so I had said,
Squealing for cookies, kinned by poor pretense
With a noble house. But the little man quite dead,
I see the forbears' antique lineaments.

The elder men have strode by the box of death
To the wide flag porch, and muttering low send round
The bruit of the day. O friendly waste of breath!
Their hearts are hurt with a deep dynastic wound.

He was pale and little, the foolish neighbors say;
The first-fruits, saith the Preacher, the Lord hath taken;
But this was the old tree's late branch wrenched away,
Grieving the sapless limbs, the shorn and shaken.

Spectral Lovers

By night they haunted a thicket of April mist,
Out of that black ground suddenly come to birth,
Else angels lost in each other and fallen on earth.
Lovers they knew they were, but why unclasped, un-
      kissed?
Why should two lovers go frozen apart in fear?
And yet they were, they were.

Over the shredding of an April blossom
Scarcely her fingers touched him, quick with care,
Yet of evasions even she made a snare.
The heart was bold that clanged within her bosom,
The moment perfect, the time stopped for them,
Still her face turned from him.

Strong were the batteries of the April night
And the stealthy emanations of the field;
Should the walls of her prison undefended yield
And open her treasure to the first clamorous knight?
"This is the mad moon, and shall I surrender all?
If he but ask it I shall."

And gesturing largely to the moon of Easter,
Mincing his steps and swishing the jubilant grass,
Beheading some field-flowers that had come to pass,
He had reduced his tributaries faster
Had not considerations pinched his heart
Unfitly for his art.

"Am I reeling with the sap of April like a drunkard?
Blessed is he that taketh this richest of cities;
But it is so stainless the sack were a thousand pities.
This is that marble fortress not to be conquered,
Lest its white peace in the black flame turn to tinder
And an unutterable cinder."

They passed me once in April, in the mist.
No other season is it when one walks and discovers
Two tall and wandering, like spectral lovers,
White in the season's moon-gold and amethyst,
Who touch their quick fingers fluttering like a bird
Whose songs shall never be heard.

Agitato ma non troppo

This is what the man said,
Insisting, standing on his head.

I have a grief,
It was not stolen like a thief,
Albeit I have no bittern by the lake
To cry it up and down the brake.

None there has been like Dante's fury
When Beatrice was given him to bury;
Except, when the young heart was hit, you know
How Percy Shelley's reed sang tremolo.

"Yes, there is grief in his mind,
But where is his fair child moaning in the wind?
Where is the white frost snowing on his head?
When did he stalk and weep and not loll in his bed?"

I will be brief,
Assuredly I know my grief,
And I am shaken; but not as a leaf.

Necrological

The friar had said his paternosters duly
And scourged his limbs, and afterwards would have slept;
But with much riddling his head became unruly,
He arose, from the quiet monastery he crept.

Dawn lightened the place where the battle had been
      won.
The people were dead—it is easy he thought to die—
These dead remained, but the living all were gone,
Gone with the wailing trumps of victory.

The dead wore no rainment against the air,
Bartholomew's men had spoiled them where they fell;
In defeat the heroes' bodies were whitely bare,
The field was white like meads of asphodel.

Not all were white; some gory and fabulous
Whom the sword had pierced and then the grey wolf
      eaten;
But the brother reasoned that heroes' flesh was thus.
Flesh fails, and the postured bones lie weather-beaten.

The lords of chivalry lay prone and shattered.
The gentle and the bodyguard of yeomen;

Bartholomew's stroke went home—but little it mattered,
Bartholomew went to be stricken of other foemen.

Beneath the blue ogive of the firmament
Was a dead warrior, clutching whose mighty knees
Was a leman, who with her flame had warmed his tent,
For him enduring all men's pleasantries.

Close by the sable stream that purged the plain
Lay the white stallion and his rider thrown,
The great beast had spilled there his little brain,
And the little groin of the knight was spilled by a stone.

The youth possessed him then of a crooked blade
Deep in the belly of a lugubrious wight;
He fingered it well, and it was cunningly made;
But strange apparatus was it for a Carmelite.

Then he sat upon a hill and bowed his head
As under a riddle, and in a deep surmise
So still that he likened himself unto those dead
Whom the kites of Heaven solicited with sweet cries.

Bells for
John Whiteside's Daughter

There was such speed in her little body,
And such lightness in her footfall,
It is no wonder her brown study
Astonishes us all.

Her wars were bruited in our high window.
We looked among orchard trees and beyond
Where she took arms against her shadow,
Or harried unto the pond

The lazy geese, like a snow cloud
Dripping their snow on the green grass,
Tricking and stopping, sleepy and proud,
Who cried in goose, Alas,

For the tireless heart within the little
Lady with rod that made them rise
From their noon apple-dreams and scuttle
Goose-fashion under the skies!

But now go the bells, and we are ready,
In one house we are sternly stopped
To say we are vexed at her brown study,
Lying so primly propped.

The Tall Girl

The Queens of Hell had lissome necks to crane
At the tall girl approaching with long tread
And, when she was caught up even with them, nodded:
"If the young miss with gold hair might not disdain,
We would esteem her company over the plain,
To profit us all where the dogs will be out barking,
And we'll go by the windows where the young men are
       working
And tomorrow we will all come home again."

But the Queen of Heaven on the other side of the road
In the likeness, I hear, of a plain motherly woman
Made a wry face, despite it was so common
To be worsted by the smooth ladies of Hell,
And crisped her sweet tongue: "This never will come
       to good!
Just an old woman, my pet, that wishes you well."

First Travels of Max

In that old house for several generations
The best of the Van Vroomans was the youngest.
But even Max, in a chevroned sailor's blouse
And tawny curls far from subdued to the cap,
Had slapped old Katie and removed himself
From games for children; that was because they told
Him never never to set a wicked foot
Into Fool's Forest, where the devil dwelt.

"Become Saint Michael's sword!" said Max to the stick,
And to the stone, "Be a forty-four revolver!"
Then Max was glad that he had armed so wisely
As darker grew the wood, and shrill with silence.
All good fairies were helpless here; at night
Whipped in an inch of their lives; weeping, forbidden
To play with strange scared truant little boys
Who didn't belong there. Snakes were allowed there
And lizards and adders—people of age and evil
That lay on their bellies and whispered—no bird nor
        rabbit.
There were more rotten trees than there were sound ones.
In that wood timber was degenerate
And rotted almost faster than it grew.

There were no flowers nor apples. Too much age.
The only innocent thing in there was Max,
And even he had cursed his little sisters.

The black tarn rose up almost in his face.
It was as black and sudden as the pit
The Adversary digs in the bowels of earth;
Bubbles were on it, breath of the black beast
(Formed like a spider, white bag for entrails)
Who took that sort of blackness to inhabit
And dangle after bad men in Fool's Forest.
"Must they be bad?" said casuistical Max.
"Mightn't a good boy who stopped saying his prayers
Be allowed to slip into the spider's fingers?"
Max raised his sword—but what can swords do
Against the Prince of the Dark? Max sheathed his point
And crept around the pool.

In the middle of the wood was the Red Witch.
Max half expected her. He never imagined
To find a witch's house so dirty and foolish,
A witch with a wide bosom yellow as butter,
Or one that combed so many obscene things
From her black hair into her scarlet lap;
He never believed there would attempt to sing
The one that taught the rats to squeal and Bashan's
Bull to bellow.

"Littlest and last Van Vrooman, do you come too?"
She knew him, it appeared, would know him better,
The scarlet hulk of hell with a fat bosom
Pirouetting at the bottom of the forest.
Certainly Max had come. But he was going;
Unequal contests never being commanded
On young knights only armed in innocency.

"When I am a grown man I will come here
And cut your head off!" That was very well.
Not a true heart beating in Christendom
Could have said more, but that for the present would do.

Max went straight home, and nothing chilled him more
Than the company kept him by the witch's laugh
And the witch's song, and the creeping of his flesh.

Max is more firmly domiciliated.
A great house is Van Vrooman, a green slope
South to the sun do the great ones inhabit,
And a few children play on the lawn with the nurse.
Max has returned to his play, and you may find him,
His famous curls unsmoothed, if you will call
Where the Van Vroomans live; the tribe Van Vrooman
Live there at least when any are at home.

Good Ships

Fleet ships encountering on the high seas
Who speak, and then unto the vast diverge,
These hailed each other, poised on the loud surge
Of one of Mrs. Grundy's Tuesday teas,
Nor trimmed one sail to baffle the driving breeze.
A macaroon absorbed all her emotion;
His hue was ashy but an effect of ocean;
They exchanged the nautical technicalities.

It was only a nothing or so, and thus they parted.
Away they sailed, most certainly bound for port,
So seaworthy one felt they could not sink;
Still there was a tremor shook them, I should think,
Beautiful timbers fit for storm and sport
And unto miserly merchant hulks converted.

Emily Hardcastle, Spinster

We shall come tomorrow morning, who were not to have
  her love,
We shall bring no face of envy but a gift of praise and
  lilies
To the stately ceremonial we are not the heroes of.

Let the sisters now attend her, who are red-eyed, who are
  wroth;
They were younger, she was finer, for they wearied of the
  waiting
And they married them to merchants, being unbelievers
  both.

I was dapper when I dangled in my pepper-and-salt;
We were only local beauties, and we beautifully trusted
If the proud one had to tarry we would have her by de-
  fault.

But right across her threshold has her Grizzled Baron
  come;
Let them wrap her as a princess, who'd go softly down a
  stairway
And seal her to the stranger for his castle in the gloom.

Parting at Dawn

If there was a broken whispering by night
It was an image of the coward heart,
But the white dawn assures them how to part—
Stoics are born on the cold glitter of light,
And with the morning star lovers take flight.
Say then your parting; and most dry should you drain
Your lips of their wine, your eyes of the frantic rain,
Till these be as the barren cenobite.

And then? O dear Sir, stumbling down the street,
Continue, till you come to wars and wounds;
Beat the air, Madam, till your house-clock sounds;
And if no Lethe flows beneath your casement,
And when ten years have not brought full effacement,
Philosophy was wrong, and you may meet.

Vaunting Oak

He is a tower unleaning. But how will he not break,
If Heaven assault him with full wind and sleet,
And what uproar tall trees concumbent make!

More than a hundred years, more than a hundred feet
Naked he rears against the cold skies eruptive;
Only his temporal twigs are unsure of seat,

And the frail leaves of a season, which are susceptive
Of the mad humors of wind, and turn and flee
In panic round the stem on which they are captive.

Now a certain heart, too young and mortally
Linked with an unbeliever of bitter blood,
Observed, as an eminent witness of life, the tree,

And exulted, wrapped in a phantasy of good:
"Be the great oak for its long winterings
Our love's symbol, better than the summer's brood."

Then the venerable oak, delivered of his pangs,
Put forth profuse his green banners of peace
And testified to her with innumerable tongues.

And what but she fetch me up to the steep place
Where the oak vaunted? A flat where birdsong flew
Had to be traversed; and a quick populace

Of daisies, and yellow kinds; and here she knew,
Who had been instructed of much mortality,
Better than brag in this distraught purlieu.

Above the little and their dusty tombs was he
Standing, sheer on his hill, not much soiled over
By the knobs and broken boughs of an old tree,

And she murmured, "Established, you see him there!
        forever."
But, that her pitiful error be undone,
I knocked on his house loudly, a sorrowing lover,

And drew forth like a funeral a hollow tone.
"The old gentleman," I grieved, "holds gallantly,
But before our joy shall have lapsed, even, will be gone."

I knocked more sternly, and his dolorous cry
Boomed till its loud reverberance outsounded
The singing of bees; or the coward birds that fly

Otherwhere with their songs when summer is sped,
And if they stayed would perish miserably;
Or the tears of a girl remembering her dread.

In Process of a Noble Alliance

Reduce this lady unto marble quickly,
Ray her beauty on a glassy plate,
Rhyme her youth at fast as the granite,
Take her where she trembles and do not wait,
For now in funeral white they lead her
And crown her queen of the House of No Love:
A dirge then for her beauty, musicians!
Not harping the springe that catches the dove.

Spiel of the Three Mountebanks

THE SWARTHY ONE—

    Villagers who gather round,
    This is Fides, my lean hound.
    Bring your bristled village curs
    To try his fang and tooth, sweet sirs!
    He will rend them, he is savage,
    Thinking nothing but to ravage,
    Nor with cudgel, fire, rope,
    May ye control my misanthrope;
    He would tear the moon in the sky
    And fly at Heaven, could he fly.
    And for his ravening without cease
    I have had of him no peace;
    Only once I bared the knife
    To quit my devil of his life,
    But listen, how I heard him say,
    "Think you I shall die today?
    Since your mother cursed and died,
    I am keeping at your side,
    We are firmly knit together,
    Two ends tugging at one tether,
    And you shall see when I shall die
    That you are mortal even as I."

Bring your stoutest-hearted curs
If ye would risk him, gentle sirs.

THE THICK ONE—

Countrymen, here's a noble frame,
Humphrey is my elephant's name.
When my father's back was bent
Under steep impediment,
Humphrey came to my possession,
With patient strength for all his passion.
Have ye a mountain to remove?
It is Humphrey's dearest love.
Pile his burden to the skies,
Loose a pestilence of flies,
Foot him in the quick morass
Where no laden beast can pass,
He will staunch his weariless back
And march unswerving on the track.
Have ye seen a back so wide,
So impenetrable hide?
Nor think ye by this Humphrey hill
Prince Hamlet bare his fardels ill?
Myself I like it not for us
To wear beneath an incubus,
I take offence, but in no rage
May I dispose my heritage;
Though in good time the vast and tough
Shall sink and totter fast enough.
So pile your population up,
They are a drop in Humphrey's cup;
Add all your curses to his pack
To make one straw for Humphrey's back.

THE PALE ONE—

If ye remark how poor I am,

23

Come, citizens, behold my lamb!
Have ye a lion, ounce, or scourge,
Or any beast of dainty gorge?
Agnus lays his tender youth
Between the very enemy's mouth.
And though he sniff his delicate meat
He may not bruise that flesh nor eat.
He may not rend him limb from limb
If Agnus do but bleat on him.
Fierce was my youth, but like a dream
I saw a temple and a stream,
And where I knelt and washed my sore,
This infant lamb stood on the shore,
He mounted with me from the river,
And still he cries, as brave as ever:
"Lay me down by the lion's side
To match my frailty with his pride.
Fain would I welter in my blood
To teach these lions true lionhood."
So daily Agnus would be slain
But daily is denied again,
And still the hungry lions range
While Agnus waits upon a change;
Only the coursing lions die
And in their deserts mortify.
So bring us lion, leopard, bear,
To try of Agnus without fear,
And ye less gentle than I am,
Come, be instructed of my Lamb.

Here Lies a Lady

Here lies a lady of beauty and high degree.
Of chills and fever she died, of fever and chills,
The delight of her husband, her aunt, an infant of three,
And of medicos marveling sweetly on her ills.

For either she burned, and her confident eyes would
      blaze,
And her fingers fly in a manner to puzzle their heads —
What was she making? Why, nothing; she sat in a maze
Of old scraps of laces, snipped into curious shreds—

Or this would pass, and the light of her fire decline
Till she lay discouraged and cold, like a thin stalk white
      and blown,
And would not open her eyes, to kisses, to wine;
The sixth of these states was her last; the cold settled
      down.

Sweet ladies, long may ye bloom, and toughly I hope
      ye may thole,
But was she not lucky? In flowers and lace and mourn-
      ing,
In love and great honor we bade God rest her soul
After six little spaces of chill, and six of burning.

The Vanity of
the Bright Young Men

You think in my tight black coat I'm like a beetle.
I never mind my looks,
I'm removed, a boy reported not liking people,
My familiars mostly are books.

I go alone to assembly, but I'd go pushing
Even to say my prayers,
Glaring with cold grey eyes at whom I am brushing,
Who would if they could with theirs.

But afternoons I walk in the primal creation,
In a spell, in a possible glory,
Counting on Nature to give me an intimation
Of my unlikely story.

One time I went, by the luck of my chances and choices,
Past certain Druid trees
Whose leaves were ears and tongues translating the voices
Hid in the muffling breeze.

Against me the counsels of spirits were not then darkened
Though out of my vision or reach,
As I set my boots to the path beneath and hearkened
Unto phrases of English speech.

One said, "This worm of the dust—he is strangely other
Than he and they suppose"—
But one, "Yet sired by his father and dammed by his
      mother?
Has he not acknowledged those?"

Again, "But wait—this man is a changeling but knows
      not—
I tell you this is a Prince"—
"From a far great kingdom and should return but goes
      not?"
"Fifteen long winters since"—

But like a King I was bound to a King's condition.
I steadied and marched right on,
Not testing by eavesdrop the wonder of my suspicion,
And quick that talk was gone.

And prompt I showed, as the tower's last throb appointed,
In the loud and litten room,
Nor was hailed by that love that leaps to the Heir
      Anointed:
"Hush, O hush, he is come."

Conrad in Twilight

Conrad, Conrad, aren't you old
To sit so late in your mouldy garden?
And I think Conrad knows it well,
Nursing his knees, too rheumy and cold
To warm the wraith of a Forest of Arden.

Neuralgia in the back of his neck,
His lungs filling with such miasma,
His feet dipping in leafage and muck:
Conrad! you've forgotten asthma.

Conrad's house has thick red walls,
The log on Conrad's hearth is blazing,
Slippers and pipe and tea are served,
Butter and toast are meant for pleasing!
Still Conrad's back is not uncurved
And here's an autumn on him, teasing.

Autumn days in our section
Are the most used-up thing on earth
(Or in the waters under the earth)
Having no more color nor predilection
Than cornstalks too wet for the fire,
A ribbon rotting on the byre,
A man's face as weathered as straw
By the summer's flare and winter's flaw.

Armageddon

Antichrist, playing his lissome flute and merry
As was his wont, debouched upon the plain;
Then came a swirl of dust, and Christ drew rein,
Brooding upon his frugal breviary.

Now which shall die, the roundel, rose, and hall,
Or else the tonsured beadsman's monkery?
For Christ and Antichrist arm cap-a-pie,
The prospect charms the soul of the lean jackal.

But Antichrist got down from the Barbary beast
And doffed his plume in courteous prostration;
Christ left his jennet's back in deprecation
And raised him, his own hand about the waist.

Then next they fingered chivalry's quaint page,
Of precedence discoursing by the letter.
The oratory of Antichrist was better,
He invested Christ with the elder lineage.

He set Christ on his own Mahomet's back
Where Christ sat fortressed up like Diomede;
The cynical hairy jennet was his steed,
Obtuse, and most indifferent to attack.

29

The lordings measured lances and stood still,
And each was loath to let the other's blood;
Originally they were one brotherhood;
There stood the white pavilion on the hill.

To the pavilion went then the hierarchs,
If they might truce their honorable dispute;
Firm was the Christian's chin and he was mute,
And Antichrist ejected scant remarks.

Antichrist tendered a spray of rosemary
To serve his brother for a buttonhole;
Then Christ about his adversary's poll
Wrapped a dry palm that grew on Calvary.

Christ wore a dusty cassock, and the knight
Did him the honors of his tiring-hall,
Whence Christ did not come forth too finical,
But his egregious beauty richly dight.

With feasting they concluded every day,
And when the other shaped his phrases thicker
Christ, introducing water in the liquor,
Made wine of more ethereal bouquet.

At wassail Antichrist would pitch the strain
For unison of all the retinue;
Christ beat the time, and hummed a stave or two,
But did not say the words, which were profane.

Perruquiers were privily presented,
Till, knowing his need extreme and his heart pure,
Christ let them dress him his thick chevelure,
And soon his beard was glozed and sweetly scented.

And so the Wolf said Brother to the Lamb,
The True Heir keeping with the poor Impostor,
The rubric and the holy paternoster
Were jangled strangely with the dithyramb.

It could not be. There was a patriarch,
A godly liege of old malignant brood,
Who could not fathom the new brotherhood
Between the children of the light and dark.

He sought the ear of Christ on these strange things,
But in the white pavilion when he stood,
And saw them favored and dressed like twins at food,
Profound and mad became his misgivings.

The voices, and their burdens, he must hear,
But equal between the pleasant Princes flew
Theology, the arts, the old customs and the new;
Hoarsely he ran and hissed in the wrong ear.

He was discomfited, but Christ much more.
Christ sheds unmannerly his devil's pelf,
Takes ashes from the hearth and smears himself,
Calls for his smock and jennet as before.

His trump recalls his own to right opinions,
With scourge they mortify their carnal selves,
With stone they whet the ax-heads on the helves
And seek the Prince Beelzebub and minions.

Christ and his myrmidons, Christ at the head,
Chanted of death and glory and no complaisance;
Antichrist and the armies of malfeasance
Made songs of innocence and no bloodshed.

The immortal Adversary shook his head:
If now they fought too long, then he would famish;
And if much blood was shed, why, he was squeamish:
"These Armageddons weary me much," he said.

Prometheus in Straits

Windy gentlemen wreathing a long verandah,
With tongues at the moments between illicit potations
Assailing all the acta and/or agenda
Of previous and/or present administrations:
Observe me carefully jotting no memoranda
Lest I seem to identify *your* wits with your nation's.

But now approaches a radiant band all spinster
Of spirits weaving delirious rhythm of chatter
About old picture galleries and Westminster;
My sensitivity's out of this world, it is utter;
I wish I were a patriarch jungle monster;
The parrots' bonnets, yes; but stop the twitter.

To the colleges then and the modern masterpieces?
Not now though I risk the damage of your inference;
Before your explications respect ceases
For the centers lost in so absurd circumference;
You have only betrayed them by your exegesis
And provoke me to gestures not of deference.

Though I be Prometheus my mind may have wandered
To bring my pious offices to this people;

Where all must be teachers nullity is engendered
And doctrine perishes crying for an ear which is simple;
The prophet is solicited before he has well thundered
And escapes with credit if he do not turn disciple.

At least my function concerns itself with this planet
And the due distinctions of faith and fact and fiction;
I will go somewhere by a streamside abounding with
          granite
And but little human history and dereliction;
To the Unknown Man I will raise an altar upon it
And comfort my knees with bruises of genuflection.

Judith of Bethulia

Beautiful as the flying legend of some leopard
She had not yet chosen her great captain or prince
Depositary to her flesh, and our defense;
And a wandering beauty is a blade out of its scabbard.
You know how dangerous, gentlemen of threescore?
May you know it yet ten more.

Nor by process of voiling she grew the less fabulous.
Grey or blue veils, we were desperate to study
The invincible emanations of her white body,
And the winds at her ordered raiment were ominous.
Might she walk in the market, sit in the council of sol-
        diers?
Only of the extreme elders.

But a rare chance was the girl's then, when the Invader
Trumpeted from the south, and rumbled from the north,
Beleaguered the city from four quarters of the earth,
Our soldiery too craven and sick to aid her—
Where were the arms could countervail this horde?
Her beauty was the sword.

She sat with the elders, and proved on their blear visage
How bright was the weapon unrusted in her keeping,

While he lay surfeiting on their harvest heaping,
Wasting the husbandry of their rarest vintage—
And dreaming of the broad-breasted dames for con-
     cubine?
These floated on his wine.

He was lapped with bay-leaves, and grass and fumiter
     weed,
And from under the wine-film encountered his mortal
     vision,
For even within his tent she accomplished his derision;
She loosed one veil and another, standing unafraid;
And he perished. Nor brushed her with even so much as a
     daisy?
She found his destruction easy.

The heathen are all perished. The victory was furnished,
We smote them hiding in our vineyards, barns, annexes,
And now their white bones clutter the holes of foxes,
And the chieftain's head, with grinning sockets, and var-
     nished—
Is it hung on the sky with a hideous epitaphy?
No, the woman keeps the trophy.

May God send unto our virtuous lady her prince.
It is stated she went reluctant to that orgy,
Yet a madness fevers our young men, and not the clergy
Nor the elders have turned them unto modesty since.
Inflamed by the thought of her naked beauty with desire?
Yes, and chilled with fear and despair.

Blue Girls

Twirling your blue skirts, travelling the sward
Under the towers of your seminary,
Go listen to your teachers old and contrary
Without believing a word.

Tie the white fillets then about your hair
And think no more of what will come to pass
Than bluebirds that go walking on the grass
And chattering on the air.

Practise your beauty, blue girls, before it fail;
And I will cry with my loud lips and publish
Beauty which all our power shall never establish,
It is so frail.

For I could tell you a story which is true;
I know a lady with a terrible tongue,
Blear eyes fallen from blue,
All her perfections tarnished—yet it is not long
Since she was lovelier than any of you.

Philomela

Procne, Philomela, and Itylus,
Your names are liquid, your improbable tale
Is recited in the classic numbers of the nightingale.
Ah, but our numbers are not felicitous,
It goes not liquidly for us.

Perched on a Roman ilex, and duly apostrophized,
The nightingale descanted unto Ovid;
She has even appeared to the Teutons, the swilled and
gravid;
At Fontainebleau it may be the bird was gallicized;
Never was she baptized.

To England came Philomela with her pain,
Fleeing the hawk her husband; querulous ghost,
She wanders when he sits heavy on his roost,
Utters herself in the original again,
The untranslatable refrain.

Not to these shores she came! this other Thrace,
Environ barbarous to the royal Attic;
How could her delicate dirge run democratic,
Delivered in a cloudless boundless public place
To an inordinate race?

I pernoctated with the Oxford students once,
And in the quadrangles, in the cloisters, on the Cher,
Precociously knocked at antique doors ajar,
Fatuously touched the hems of the hierophants,
Sick of my dissonance.

I went out to Bagley Wood, I climbed the hill;
Even the moon had slanted off in a twinkling,
I heard the sepulchral owl and a few bells tinkling,
There was no more villainous day to unfulfil,
The diuturnity was still.

Up from the darkest wood where Philomela sat,
Her fairy numbers issued. What then ailed me?
My ears are called capacious but they failed me,
Her classics registered a little flat!
I rose, and venomously spat.

Philomela, Philomela, lover of song,
I am in despair if we may make us worthy,
A bantering breed sophistical and swarthy;
Unto more beautiful, persistently more young,
Thy fabulous provinces belong.

Old Man Playing with Children

A discreet householder exclaims on the grandsire
In warpaint and feathers, with fierce grandsons and axes
Dancing round a backyard fire of boxes:
"Watch grandfather, he'll set the house on fire."

But I will unriddle for you the thought of his mind,
An old one you cannot open with conversation.
What animates the thin legs in risky motion?
Mixes the snow on the head with snow on the wind?

"Grandson, grandsire. We are equally boy and boy.
Do not offer your reclining-chair and slippers
With tedious old women talking in wrappers.
This life is not good but in danger and in joy.

"It is you the elder to these and younger to me
Who are penned as slaves by properties and causes
And never walk from your insupportable houses
And shamefully, when boys shout, go in and flee.

"May God forgive me, I know your middling ways,
Having taken care and performed ignominies un-
        reckoned
Between the first brief childhood and the brief second,
But I will be more honorable in these days."

Captain Carpenter

Captain Carpenter rose up in his prime
Put on his pistols and went riding out
But had got wellnigh nowhere at that time
Till he fell in with ladies in a rout.

It was a pretty lady and all her train
That played with him so sweetly but before
An hour she'd taken a sword with all her main
And twined him of his nose for evermore.

Captain Carpenter mounted up one day
And rode straightway into a stranger rogue
That looked unchristian but be that as may
The Captain did not wait upon prologue.

But drew upon him out of his great heart
The other swung against him with a club
And cracked his two legs at the shinny part
And let him roll and stick like any tub.

Captain Carpenter rode many a time
From male and female took he sundry harms
He met the wife of Satan crying "I'm
The she-wolf bids you shall bear no more arms."

Their strokes and counters whistled in the wind
I wish he had delivered half his blows
But where she should have made off like a hind
The bitch bit off his arms at the elbows.

And Captain Carpenter parted with his ears
To a black devil that used him in this wise
O Jesus ere his threescore and ten years
Another had plucked out his sweet blue eyes.

Captain Carpenter got up on his roan
And sallied from the gate in hell's despite
I heard him asking in the grimmest tone
If any enemy yet there was to fight?

"To any adversary it is fame
If he risk to be wounded by my tongue
Or burnt in two beneath my red heart's flame
Such are the perils he is cast among.

"But if he can he has a pretty choice
From an anatomy with little to lose
Whether he cut my tongue and take my voice
Or whether it be my round red heart he choose."

It was the neatest knave that ever was seen
Stepping in perfume from his lady's bower
Who at this word put in his merry mien
And fell on Captain Carpenter like a tower.

I would not knock old fellows in the dust
But there lay Captain Carpenter on his back
His weapons were the old heart in his bust
And a blade shook between rotten teeth alack.

The rogue in scarlet and grey soon knew his mind
He wished to get his trophy and depart
With gentle apology and touch refined
He pierced him and produced the Captain's heart.

God's mercy rest on Captain Carpenter now
I thought him Sirs an honest gentleman
Citizen husband soldier and scholar enow
Let jangling kites eat of him if they can.

But God's deep curses follow after those
That shore him of his goodly nose and ears
His legs and strong arms at the two elbows
And eyes that had not watered seventy years.

The curse of hell upon the sleek upstart
That got the Captain finally on his back
And took the red red vitals of his heart
And made the kites to whet their beaks clack clack.

Old Mansion

As an intruder I trudged with careful innocence
To mask in decency a meddlesome stare,
Passing the old house often on its eminence,
Exhaling my foreign weed on its weighted air.

Here age seemed newly imaged for the historian
After his monstrous châteaux on the Loire,
A beauty not for depicting by old vulgarian
Reiterations that gentle readers abhor.

It was a Southern manor. One hardly imagines
Towers, arcades, or forbidding fortress walls;
But sufficient state though its peacocks now were pigeons;
Where no courts kept, but grave rites and funerals.

Indeed, not distant, possibly not external
To the property, were tombstones, where the catafalque
Had carried their dead; and projected a note too charnel
But for the honeysuckle on its intricate stalk.

Stability was the character of its rectangle
Whose line was seen in part and guessed in part

Through trees. Decay was the tone of old brick and
        shingle.
Green shutters dragging frightened the watchful heart

To assert: Your mansion, long and richly inhabited,
Its porches and bowers suiting the children of men,
Will not for ever be thus, O man, exhibited,
And one had best hurry to enter it if one can.

And at last, with my happier angel's own temerity,
Did I clang their brazen knocker against the door,
To beg their dole of a look, in simple charity,
Or crumbs of wisdom dropping from their great store.

But it came to nothing—and may so gross denial
Which has been deplored with a beating of the breast
Never shorten the tired historian, loyal
To acknowledge defeat and discover a new quest.

The old mistress was ill, and sent my dismissal
By one even more wrappered and lean and dark
Than that warped concierge and imperturbable vassal
Who had bid me begone from her master's Gothic park.

Emphatically, the old house crumbled; the ruins
Would litter, as already the leaves, this petted sward;
And no annalist went in to the lords or the peons;
The antiquary would finger the bits of shard.

But on retreating I saw myself in the token,
How loving from my dying weed the feather curled
On the languid air; and I went with courage shaken
To dip, alas, into some unseemlier world.

Piazza Piece

—I am a gentleman in a dustcoat trying
To make you hear. Your ears are soft and small
And listen to an old man not at all,
They want the young men's whispering and sighing.
But see the roses on your trellis dying
And hear the spectral singing of the moon;
For I must have my lovely lady soon,
I am a gentleman in a dustcoat trying.

—I am a lady young in beauty waiting
Until my truelove comes, and then we kiss.
But what grey man among the vines is this
Whose words are dry and faint as in a dream?
Back from my trellis, Sir, before I scream!
I am a lady young in beauty waiting.

Eclogue

JANE SNEED BEGAN IT: My poor John, alas,
Ten years ago, pretty it was in a ring
To run as boys and girls do in the grass—
At that time leap and hollo and skip and sing
Came easily to pass.

And precious little innocents were we,
Said a boy, "Now shall we let her be the fox?"
Or a girl, "Now which of you will climb the tree?"
We were quick-foot the deer, strong-back the ox,
We were the busy bee.

JOHN BLACK SAID: I'll interpret what you mean.
Our infant selves played happily with our others,
The cunning me and mine came not between
Which like a sword is, O sweethearts and brothers
Numberless, who have seen.

JANE SNEED: I tell you what I used to do.
For joy I used to run by river or wood
To see with what speed all came trooping too;
Those days I could not quit you if I would,
Nor yet quit me could you.

JOHN BLACK RETURNED: But now, Jane, it appears
We are sly travelers, keeping good lookout
Against the face whose ravage cries for tears;
Old friends, ill met; and supposing I call out,
"Draw nigh, friend of these years"—

Before he think of any reason why,
The features of that man resolve and burn
For one long look—but then the flame must die.
The cold hearts in us mortally return,
We must not fructify.

JANE SNEED SAID BITTERLY: Why, John, you are right.
We were spendthrifts of joy when we were young,
But we became usurious, and in fright
Conceived that such a waste of days was wrong
For marchers unto night.

JOHN BLACK SAID: Yes, exactly, that was when
It happened. For Time involved us: in his toils
We learned to fear. And every day since then
We are mortals teasing for immortal spoils,
Desperate women and men.

JANE SNEED CONSENTED: It was nothing but this.
Love suffereth long, is kind—but not in fear.
For boys run banded, and simple sweethearts kiss,
Till in one day the dream of Death appear—
Then metamorphosis.

JOHN BLACK SAID: To explain mistrust and wars,
Theogony has a black witch with hell's broth;
Or a preposterous marriage of fleshless stars;
Or the Fiend's own naked person; or God wroth
Fingering his red scars.

48

And philosophy, an art of equal worth,
Tells of a flaw in the firmament—spots in the sun—
A Third Day's error when the upheaving earth
Was young and prime—a Fate reposed upon
The born before their birth.

JANE SNEED WITH GRIM LIPS MOCKED HIM: Who can
   tell—
Not I, not you—about those mysteries!
Something, John Black, came flapping out of hell
And wrought between us, and the chasm is
Digged, and it digged it well.

JOHN BLACK IN DEPRECATION SAID: Be sure
That love has suffered a most fatal eclipse;
All brotherhoods, filialities insecure;
Lovers compounding honey on their lips
With deep doubts to endure.

JANE SNEED SIGHED SLOWLY: I suppose it stands
Just so. Yet I can picture happiness—
Perhaps there wander lovers in some lands
Who when Night comes, when it is fathomless,
Consort their little hands;

And well, John Black the darkened lovers may,
The hands hold much of heat in little storage,
The eyes are almost torches good as day,
And one flame to the other flame cries Courage,
When heart to heart slide they;

So they keep unafraid the whole night through,
Till the sun of a sudden glowing through the bushes
They wake and laugh, their eyes again are blue,

And listen! are those not the doves, the thrushes?
Look there! the golden dew.

JOHN BLACK'S THE LAST SAY THEN: O innocent dove,
This is a dream. We lovers mournfully
Exchange our bleak despairs. We are one part love
And nine parts bitter thought. As well might be
Beneath ground as above.

Vision by Sweetwater

Go and ask Robin to bring the girls over
To Sweetwater, said my Aunt; and that was why
It was like a dream of ladies sweeping by
The willows, clouds, deep meadowgrass, and the river.

Robin's sisters and my Aunt's lily daughter
Laughed and talked, and tinkled light as wrens
If there were a little colony all hens
To go walking by the steep turn of Sweetwater.

Let them alone, dear Aunt, just for one minute
Till I go fishing in the dark of my mind:
Where have I seen before, against the wind,
These bright virgins, robed and bare of bonnet,

Flowing with music of their strange quick tongue
And adventuring with delicate paces by the stream,—
Myself a child, old suddenly at the scream
From one of the white throats which it hid among?

Her Eyes

To a woman that I knew
Were eyes of an extravagant hue:
V*iz.*, china blue.

Those I wear upon my head
Are sometimes green and sometimes red,
I said.

My mother's eyes are wet and blear,
My little sister's are not clear,
Poor silly dear.

It must be given to but few,
A pair of eyes so utter blue
And new;

Where does she keep them from this glare
Of the monstrous sun and the wind's flare
Without any wear;

And were they never in the night
Poisoned by artificial light
Much too bright;

And had the splendid beast no heart
That boiled with tears and baked with smart
The ocular part?

I'll have no business with those eyes,
They are not kind, they are not wise,
They are two great lies.

A woman shooting such blue flame
I apprehend will get some blame
On her good name.

Parting, without a Sequel

She has finished and sealed the letter
At last, which he so richly has deserved,
With characters venomous and hatefully curved,
And nothing could be better.

But even as she gave it
Saying to the blue-capped functioner of doom,
"Into his hands," she hoped the leering groom
Might somewhere lose and leave it.

Then all the blood
Forsook the face. She was too pale for tears,
Observing the ruin of her younger years.
She went and stood

Under her father's vaunting oak
Who kept his peace in wind and sun, and glistened
Stoical in the rain; to whom she listened
If he spoke.

And now the agitation of the rain
Rasped his sere leaves, and he talked low and gentle

Reproaching the wan daughter by the lintel;
Ceasing and beginning again.

Away went the messenger's bicycle,
His serpent's track went up the hill forever,
And all the time she stood there hot as fever
And cold as any icicle.

Hilda

I

The dearest was the one to whom it fell
To walk and wear her beauty as in a play
To be enacted nobly on a great day;
And stormily we approved the bosom-swell,
And the tones tinkling. For her touch and smell
I brought bright flowers, till garlanded she stood
Scared with her splendor, as in the sight of God
A pale girl curtsying with an asphodel.

No, No, she answered in the extreme of fear,
I cannot. On the dropping of those petals
Rode the Estranger, scorning their sweet mettles,
Blossoms and woman too; him she looked at,
Not me the praiser; she was too honest for that,
I was a clod mumbling, to catch her ear.

II

The perished were the fairest. And now uprise
Particular ghosts, who hollow and clamorous
Come as blanched lepers crying, "Do not spurn us,"
Ringing in my ears, wetting my eyes,

Obsequious phantoms and disbodied sighs.
Soon they are frightened and go fast; a smoke
Which clung about my quincebushes, then broke,
And while I look is smeared upon the skies.

But Hilda! proudest, lingering last alone,
Wreathing my roses with blue bitter dust,
Think not I would reject you, for I must
Weep for your nakedness and no retinue,
And leap up as of old to follow you;
But what I wear is flesh; it weighs like stone.

Janet Waking

Beautifully Janet slept
Till it was deeply morning. She woke then
And thought about her dainty-feathered hen,
To see how it had kept.

One kiss she gave her mother.
Only a small one gave she to her daddy
Who would have kissed each curl of his shining baby;
No kiss at all for her brother.

"Old Chucky, old Chucky!" she cried,
Running across the world upon the grass
To Chucky's house, and listening. But alas,
Her Chucky had died.

It was a transmogrifying bee
Came droning down on Chucky's old bald head
And sat and put the poison. It scarcely bled,
But how exceedingly

And purply did the knot
Swell with the venom and communicate
Its rigor! Now the poor comb stood up straight
But Chucky did not.

So there was Janet
Kneeling on the wet grass, crying her brown hen
(Translated far beyond the daughters of men)
To rise and walk upon it.

And weeping fast as she had breath
Janet implored us, "Wake her from her sleep!"
And would not be instructed in how deep
Was the forgetful kingdom of death.

Lady Lost

This morning, flew up the lane
A timid lady bird to our birdbath
And eyed her image dolefully as death;
This afternoon, knocked on our windowpane
To be let in from the rain.

And when I caught her eye
She looked aside, but at the clapping thunder
And sight of the whole world blazing up like tinder
Looked in on us again most miserably,
Indeed as if she would cry.

So I will go out into the park and say,
"Who has lost a delicate brown-eyed lady
In the West End section? Or has anybody
Injured some fine woman in some dark way
Last night, or yesterday?

"Let the owner come and claim possession,
No questions will be asked. But stroke her gently
With loving words, and she will evidently
Return to her full soft-haired white-breasted fashion
And her right home and her right passion."

Two in August

Two that could not have lived their single lives
As can some husbands and wives
Did something strange: they tensed their vocal cords
And attacked each other with silences and words
Like catapulted stones and arrowed knives.

Dawn was not yet; night is for loving or sleeping,
Sweet dreams or safekeeping;
Yet he of the wide brows that were used to laurel
And she, the famed for gentleness, must quarrel.
Furious both of them, and scared, and weeping.

How sleepers groan, twitch, wake to such a mood
Is not well understood,
Nor why two entities grown almost one
Should rend and murder trying to get undone,
With individual tigers in their blood.

She in terror fled from the marriage chamber
Circuiting the dark rooms like a string of amber
Round and round and back,
And would not light one lamp against the black,
And heard the clock that clanged: Remember, Remember.

And he must tread barefooted the dim lawn,
Soon he was up and gone;
High in the trees the night-mastered birds were crying
With fear upon their tongues, no singing nor flying
Which are their lovely attitudes by dawn.

Whether those bird-cries were of heaven or hell
There is no way to tell;
In the long ditch of darkness the man walked
Under the hackberry trees where the birds talked
With words too sad and strange to syllable.

Persistent Explorer

The noise of water teased his literal ears
Which heard the distant drumming and thus scored:
Water is falling—it fell—therefore it roared.
However: That is more than water I hear!

He went still higher, and on the dizzy brink
His eyes confirmed with vision what he had heard:
This is but tumbling water. Again he demurred:
That was not only water flashing, I think.

But listen as he might, look fast or slow,
It was water, only water, tons of it
Dropping into the gorge, and every bit
Was water—the insipid chemical H_2O.

Its thunder smote him somewhat as the loud
Words of the god that rang around a man
Walking by the Mediterranean.
Its cloud of froth was whiter than the cloud

That clothed the goddess sliding down the air
Unto a mountain shepherd, white as she
That issued from the smoke refulgently.
The cloud was, but the goddess was not there.

Tremendous the sound was but there was no voice
That spoke to him. Furious the spectacle
But it spelled nothing, there was not any spell
Bidding him whether cower or rejoice.

What would he have it spell? He scarcely knew;
Only that water and nothing but water filled
His eyes and ears, nothing but water that spilled;
And if the smoke and rattle of water drew

From the deep thickets of his mind the train,
The fierce fauns and the timid tenants there,
That burst their bonds and rushed upon the air,
Why, he must turn and beat them down again.

So be it. And no unreasonable outcry
The pilgrim made; only a rueful grin
Spread over his lips until he drew them in;
He did not sit upon a rock and die.

There were many ways of dying; witness, if he
Commit himself to the water, and descend
Wrapped in the water, turn water at the end
And flow with a great water out to sea.

But there were many ways of living too,
And let his enemies gibe, but let them say
That he would throw this continent away
And seek another country,—as he would do.

Morning

Jane awoke Ralph so gently on one morning
That first, before the true householder Learning
Came back to tenant in the haunted head,
He lay upon his back and let his stare
Penetrate dazedly into the blue air
That swam all round his bed,
And in the blessed silence nothing was said.

Then his eyes travelled through the window
And lit, enchantedly, on such a meadow
Of wings and light and clover,
He would propose to Jane then to go walking
Through the green waves, and to be singing not talking;
Such imps were pranking over
Him helpless lying in bed beneath a cover.

Suddenly he remembered about himself,
His manliness returned entire to Ralph;
The dutiful mills of the brain
Began to whir with their smooth-grinding wheels
And the sly visitors wriggled off like eels;
He rose and was himself again.
Simply another morning, and simply Jane.

Somewhere Is Such a Kingdom

The famous kingdom of the birds
Has a sweet tongue and liquid words,
The red-birds polish their notes
In their easy practised throats.
Smooth as orators are the thrushes
Of the airy city of the bushes,
And God reward the fierce cock wrens
Who have such suavity with their hens.

To me this has its worth
As I sit upon the earth
Lacking my winter and quiet hearth.
For I go up into a nook
With a mind burdened or a book,
And hear no strife nor quarreling
As the birds and their wives sing.

Or, so it has been today.
Yet I cannot therefore say
If the red-bird, wren, or thrush
Know when to speak and when to hush;
Though their manifest education
Be a right enunciation,

And their chief excellence
A verbal elegance.
I cannot say if the wind never blows,
Nor how it sometimes goes.

This I know, that if they wrangle,
Their words inevitably will jangle.
If they be hateful as men
They will be harsh as we have been.
When they go to pecking
You will soon hear shrieking,
And they who will have the law,
How those will jaw!
Girls that have unlawful dreams
Will waken full of their own screams,
And boys that get too arrant
Will have rows with a parent,—
And when friend falls out with friend
All songs must have quick end.

Have they not claws like knives?
Have not these gentlemen wives?

But when they croak and fleer and swear,
My dull heart I must take elsewhere;
For I will see if God has made
Otherwhere another shade
Where the men or beasts or birds
Exchange few words and pleasant words.
And dare I think it is absurd
If no such beast were, no such bird?

Old Man Pondered

Three times he crossed our way where with me went
One who is fair and gentle, and it was strange,
But not once glancing did his vision range
Wayward on me, or my most innocent,
But strictly watched his own predicament.
How are old spirits so dead? His eye seemed true
As mine, he walked by it, it was as blue,
How came it monstered in its fixed intent?

But I will venture how. In his long years
Close-watched and dangerous, many a bright-barbed hate
Burning had smote against the optic gate
To enter and destroy. But the quick gears
Blinked shut the aperture. Else those grim leers
Had won to the inner chamber where sat Hope
To spin and pray, and made her misanthrope,
And bled her courage with a thousand spears.

Thus hate and scorn. And he must guard as well
Against alluring love, whose mild engine
Was perilous too for the lone sitter-in,
So hard consented to her little cell;
The tenderest looks vainly upon him fell,

Of dearest company, lest one light arrow
Be sharpened with a most immortal sorrow.
So had he kept his mansion shut of hell.

Firm and upright he walked for one so old,
Thrice-pondered; and I dare not prophesy
What age must bring me; for I look round bold
And seek my enemies out; and leave untold
The sideway watery dog's-glances I
Send fawning on you, thinking you will not scold.

Antique Harvesters

(SCENE: *Of the Mississippi the bank sinister, and of the Ohio the bank sinister.*)

Tawny are the leaves turned but they still hold,
And it is harvest; what shall this land produce?
A meager hill of kernels, a runnel of juice;
Declension looks from our land, it is old.
Therefore let us assemble, dry, grey, spare,
And mild as yellow air.

"I hear the croak of a raven's funeral wing."
The young men would be joying in the song
Of passionate birds; their memories are not long.
What is it thus rehearsed in sable? "Nothing."
Trust not but the old endure, and shall be older
Than the scornful beholder.

We pluck the spindling ears and gather the corn.
One spot has special yield? "On this spot stood
Heroes and drenched it with their only blood."
And talk meets talk, as echoes from the horn
Of the hunter—echoes are the old men's arts,
Ample are the chambers of their hearts.

Here come the hunters, keepers of a rite;
The horn, the hounds, the lank mares coursing by
Straddled with archetypes of chivalry;
And the fox, lovely ritualist, in flight
Offering his unearthly ghost to quarry;
And the fields, themselves to harry.

Resume, harvesters. The treasure is full bronze
Which you will garner for the Lady, and the moon
Could tinge it no yellower than does this noon;
But grey will quench it shortly—the field, men, stones.
Pluck fast, dreamers; prove as you amble slowly
Not less than men, not wholly.

Bare the arm, dainty youths, bend the knees
Under bronze burdens. And by an autumn tone
As by a grey, as by a green, you will have known
Your famous Lady's image; for so have these;
And if one say that easily will your hands
More prosper in other lands,

Angry as wasp-music be your cry then:
"Forsake the Proud Lady, of the heart of fire,
The look of snow, to the praise of a dwindled choir,
Song of degenerate specters that were men?
The sons of the fathers shall keep her, worthy of
What these have done in love."

True, it is said of our Lady, she ageth.
But see, if you peep shrewdly, she hath not stooped;
Take no thought of her servitors that have drooped,
For we are nothing; and if one talk of death—
Why, the ribs of the earth subsist frail as a breath
If but God wearieth.

71

Our Two Worthies

All the here and all the there
Ring with the praises of the pair:
Jesus the Paraclete
And Saint Paul the Exegete.

Jesus proclaimed the truth.
Paul's missionary tooth
Shredded it fine, and made a paste,
No particle going to waste,
Kneaded it and caked it
And buttered it and baked it
(And indeed all but digested
While Jesus went to death and rested)
Into a marketable compound
Ready to lay on any wound,
Meet to prescribe to our distress
And feed unto our emptiness.

And this is how the Pure Idea
Became our perfect panacea,
Both external and internal
And supernal and infernal.

When the great captains die,
There is some faithful standing by
To whom the chieftain hands his sword.
Proud Paul received—a Word.

This was the man who, given his cause,
Gave constitution and by-laws,
Distinguished pedagogue
Who invaded the synagogue
And in a little while
Was proselyting the Gentile.

But what would there have been for Paul
If the Source had finished all?
He blessed the mighty Paraclete
For needing him, to miss defeat,
He couldn't have done anything
But for his Captain spiriting.

He knew that he was competent
For any sort of punishment,
With his irresistible urge
To bare his back unto the scourge,
Teasing his own neck
In prodigious shipwreck;
Hunger and rats and gaol
Were mere detail.

Paul was every inch of him
Valiant as the Seraphim,
And all he went among
Confessed his marvelous tongue,
And Satan fearing the man's spell
Embittered smote the gates of Hell.

So he finished his fight
And he too went from sight.

Then let no cantankerous schism
Corrupt this our catechism
But one and all let us repeat:
Who then is Jesus?
He is our Paraclete.
And Paul, out of Tarsus?
He is our Exegete.

Puncture

Darkness was bad as weariness, till Grimes said,
"We've got to have a fire." But in that case
The match must sputter and the flame glare red
On nothing beautiful, and set no seal of grace
On any dead man's face.

And when the flames roared, when the sparks dartled
And quenched in the black sea that closed us round,
I looked at Grimes my dear comrade and startled
His look, blue-bright—and under it a wound
Which bled upon the ground.

"They got you? I have only lost a hat,
I would have sold the affair for three thin dimes,
But they have stuck your side. It must be looked at
And mended." "No, it's an old puncture," said Grimes,
"Which takes to bleeding sometimes."

"Why, Grimes, I never knew your mortal blood
Had wasted for my sake in scarlet streams,
And no word said. A curse on my manhood
If I knew anything! This is my luck which seems
Worse than my evillest dreams."

But when I would have comforted his white flesh
With ointment and flowing water, he said then,
"Get away. Go work on the corpses, if you wish,
Prop their heads up again, wrap their bones in,
They were good pious men.

"But as for me I have the devil's desire
For delicate tobacco in my pipe, and leisure
To stretch my toes in comfort by this fire.
Amuse yourself then some way, find some pleasure
Sleeping, or digging a treasure."

I could not find it. It was too melancholy
Sitting by Grimes my fortress who reared his head
Breached in the left wall, and subsiding slowly
To the defunctive posture of the stained dead
That now not even bled.

I, not to weep then, like a desperado
Kicked on the carcasses of our enemies
To heave them into the darkness; but my bravado
Quailed in the scorn of Grimes; for even these
Were fit for better courtesies.

Blue blazed the eyes of Grimes in the old manner—
The flames of eyes which jewel the head of youth
Were strange in the leathery phiz of the old campaigner—
Smoke and a dry word crackled from his mouth
Which a cold wind ferried south.

Dog

Cock-a-doodle-doo the brass-lined rooster says,
Brekekekex intones the fat Greek frog—
These fantasies do not terrify me as
The bow-wow-wow of dog.

I had a little doggie who used to sit and beg,
A pretty little creature with tears in his eyes
And anomalous hand extended on his leg;
Housebroken was my Huendchen, and so wise.

Booms the voice of a big dog like a bell.
But Fido sits at dusk on Madam's lap
And, bored beyond his tongue's poor skill to tell,
Rehearses his pink paradigm, To yap.

However. Up the lane the tender bull
Proceeds unto his kine; he years for them,
Whose eyes adore him and are beautiful;
Love speeds him and no treason nor mayhem.

But, on arriving at the gap in the fence,
Behold! again the ubiquitous hairy dog,
Like a numerous army rattling the battlements

With shout, though it is but his monologue,
With a lion's courage and a bee's virulence
Though he is but one dog.

Shrill is the fury of the proud red bull,
His knees quiver, and the honeysuckle vine
Expires with anguish as his voice, terrible,
Cries, "What do you want of my twenty lady kine?"

Now the air trembles to the sorrowing Moo
Of twenty blameless ladies of the mead
Fearing their lord's precarious set-to.
It is the sunset and the heavens bleed.

The hooves of the red bull slither the claybank
And cut the green tendrils of the vine; his horn
Slices the young birch unto splinter and shank
But lunging leaves the bitch's boy untorn.

Across the red sky comes master, Hodge by name,
Upright, biped, tall-browed, and self-assured,
In his hand a cudgel, in his cold eye a flame:
"Have I beat my dog so sore and he is not cured?"

His stick and stone and curse rain on the brute
That pipped his bull of gentle pedigree
Till the leonine smarts with pain and disrepute
And the bovine weeps in the bosom of his family.

Old Hodge stays not his hand, but whips to kennel
The renegade. God's peace betide the souls
Of the pure in heart! But in the box that fennel
Grows round, are two red eyes that stare like coals.

Man without
Sense of Direction

Tell this to ladies: how a hero man
Assail a thick and scandalous giant
Who casts true shadow in the sun,
And die, but play no truant.

This is more horrible: that the darling egg
Of the chosen people hatch a creature
Of noblest mind and powerful leg
Who cannot fathom nor perform his nature.

The larks' tongues are never stilled
Where the pale spread straw of sunlight lies
Then what invidious gods have willed
Him to be seized so otherwise?

Birds of the field and beasts of the stable
Are swollen with rapture and make uncouth
Demonstration of joy, which is a babble
Offending the ear of the fervorless youth.

Love—is it the cause? the proud shamed spirit?
Love has slain some whom it possessed,
But his was requited beyond his merit
And won him in bridal the loveliest.

Yet scarcely he issues from the warm chamber,
Flushed with her passion, when cold as dead
Once more he walks where waves past number
Of sorrow buffet his curse-hung head.

Whether by street, or in field full of honey,
Attended by clouds of the creatures of air
Or shouldering the city's companioning many,
His doom is on him; and how can he care

For the shapes that would fiddle upon his senses,
Wings and faces and mists that move,
Words, sunlight, the blue air which rinses
The pure pale head which he must love?

And he writhes like an antique man of bronze
That is beaten by furies visible,
Yet he is punished not knowing his sins
And for his innocence walks in hell.

He flails his arms, he moves his lips:
"Rage have I none, cause, time, nor country—
Yet I have traveled land and ships
And knelt my seasons in the chantry."

So he stands muttering; and rushes
Back to the tender thing in his charge
With clamoring tongue and taste of ashes
And a small passion to feign large.

But let his cold lips be her omen,
She shall not kiss that harried one
To peace, as men are served by women
Who comfort them in darkness and in sun.

Survey of Literature

In all the good Greek of Plato
I lack my roastbeef and potato.

A better man was Aristotle,
Pulling steady on the bottle.

I dip my hat to Chaucer,
Swilling soup from his saucer,

And to Master Shakespeare
Who wrote big on small beer.

The abstemious Wordsworth
Subsisted on a curd's-worth,

But a slick one was Tennyson,
Putting gravy on his venison.

What these men had to eat and drink
Is what we say and what we think.

The influence of Milton
Came wry out of Stilton.

Sing a song for Percy Shelley,
Drowned in pale lemon jelly,

And for precious John Keats,
Dripping blood of pickled beets.

Then there was poor Willie Blake,
He foundered on sweet cake.

God have mercy on the sinner
Who must write with no dinner,

No gravy and no grub,
No pewter and no pub,

No belly and no bowels,
Only consonants and vowels.

The Equilibrists

Full of her long white arms and milky skin
He had a thousand times remembered sin.
Alone in the press of people traveled he,
Minding her jacinth, and myrrh, and ivory.

Mouth he remembered: the quaint orifice
From which came heat that flamed upon the kiss,
Till cold words came down spiral from the head.
Grey doves from the officious tower illsped.

Body: it was a white field ready for love,
On her body's field, with the gaunt tower above,
The lilies grew, beseeching him to take,
If he would pluck and wear them, bruise and break.

Eyes talking: Never mind the cruel words,
Embrace my flowers, but not embrace the swords.
But what they said, the doves came straightway flying
And unsaid: Honor, Honor, they came crying.

Importunate her doves. Too pure, too wise,
Clambering on his shoulder, saying, Arise,
Leave me now, and never let us meet,
Eternal distance now command thy feet.

Predicament indeed, which thus discovers
Honor among thieves, Honor between lovers.
O such a little word is Honor, they feel!
But the grey word is between them cold as steel.

At length I saw these lovers fully were come
Into their torture of equilibrium;
Dreadfully had forsworn each other, and yet
They were bound each to each, and they did not forget.

And rigid as two painful stars, and twirled
About the clustered night their prison world,
They burned with fierce love always to come near,
But honor beat them back and kept them clear.

Ah, the strict lovers, they are ruined now!
I cried in anger. But with puddled brow
Devising for those gibbeted and brave
Came I descanting: Man, what would you have?

For spin your period out, and draw your breath,
A kinder saeculum begins with Death.
Would you ascend to Heaven and bodiless dwell?
Or take your bodies honorless to Hell?

In Heaven you have heard no marriage is,
No white flesh tinder to your lecheries,
Your male and female tissue sweetly shaped
Sublimed away, and furious blood escaped.

Great lovers lie in Hell, the stubborn ones
Infatuate of the flesh upon the bones;
Stuprate, they rend each other when they kiss,
The pieces kiss again, no end to this.

But still I watched them spinning, orbited nice.
Their flames were not more radiant than their ice.
I dug in the quiet earth and wrought the tomb
And made these lines to memorize their doom:—

EPITAPH

Equilibrists lie here; stranger, tread light;
Close, but untouching in each other's sight;
Mouldered the lips and ashy the tall skull.
Let them lie perilous and beautiful.

Prelude to an Evening

Do not enforce the tired wolf
Dragging his infected wound homeward
To sit tonight with the warm children
Naming the pretty kings of France.

The images of the invaded mind
Being as monsters in the dreams
Of your most brief enchanted headful,
Suppose a miracle of confusion:

That dreamed and undreamt become each other
And mix the night and day of your mind;
And it does not matter your twice crying
From mouth unbeautied against the pillow

To avert the gun of the swarthy soldier,
For cry, cock-crow, or the iron bell
Can crack the sleep-sense of outrage,
Annihilate phantoms who were nothing.

But now, by our perverse supposal,
There is a drift of fog on your mornings;
You in your peignoir, dainty at your orange-cup,
Feel poising round the sunny room

Invisible evil, deprived, and bold.
All day the clock will metronome
Your gallant fear; the needles clicking,
The heels detonating the stair's cavern.

Freshening the water in the blue bowls
For the buckberries with not all your love,
You shall be listening for the low wind,
The warning sibilance of pines.

You like a waning moon, and I accusing
Our too banded Eumenides,
You shall make Noes but wanderingly,
Smoothing the heads of the hungry children.

What Ducks Require

Ducks require no ship and sail
Bellied on the foamy skies,
Who scud north. Male and female
Make a slight nest to arise
Where they overtake the spring,
Which clogs with muddy going.

The zone unready. But the pond,
Eye of a bleak Cyclops visage, catches
Such glints of hyacinth and bland
As bloom in aquarelles of ditches
On a cold spring ground, a freak,
A weathering chance even in the wrack.

The half-householders for estate
Beam their floor with ribs of grass,
Disdain your mortises and slate
And Lar who invalided lies,
The marsh quakes dangerous, the port
Where wet and dry precisely start.

Furled, then, the quadrate wing
From the lewd eye and fowler's gun

Till in that wet sequestering,
Webtoed, the progeny is done,
Cold-hatched, the infant prodigy tries
To preen his feathers for the skies.

Prodigious in his wide degrees
Who where the winds and waters blow
On raveling banks of fissured seas
In reeds nestles, or will rise and go
Where Capicornus dips his hooves
In the blue chasm of no wharves.

Of Margaret

With the fall of the first leaf that winds rend
She and the boughs trembled, and she would mourn
The wafer body as an own first born,
But with louder destruction sang the wind.

So must the others drop, there where they hung
Quaking and cold, and the blind land be filled
With dead, till one least and last wind unchild
Her of the sons of all her mothering.

No mother sorrow is but follows birth
And, beyond that, conception; hers was large,
And so immoderate love must be a scourge,
Needing the whole ecstasy of substant earth.

But no evil shall spot this, Margaret's page,
For her generations were of the head,
The eyes, the tender fingers, not the blood,
And the issue was all flowers and foliage.

Virgin, whose image bent to the small grass
I keep against this tide of wayfaring,
O hear the maiden pageant ever sing
Of that far away time of gentleness.

Painted Head

By dark severance the apparition head
Smiles from the air a capital on no
Column or a Platonic perhaps head
On a canvas sky depending from nothing;

Stirs up an old illusion of grandeur
By tickling the instinct of heads to be
Absolute and to try decapitation
And to play truant from the body bush;

But too happy and beautiful for those sorts
Of head (homekeeping heads are happiest)
Discovers maybe thirty unwidowed years
Of not dishonoring the faithful stem;

Is nameless and has authored for the evil
Historian headhunters neither book
Nor state and is therefore distinct from tart
Heads with crowns and guilty gallery heads;

Wherefore the extravagant device of art
Unhousing by abstraction this once head
Was capital irony by a loving hand
That knew the no treason of a head like this;

Makes repentance in an unlovely head
For having vinegarly traduced the flesh
Till, the hurt flesh recusing, the hard egg
Is shrunken to its own deathlike surface;

And an image thus. The body bears the head
(So hardly one they terribly are two)
Feeds and obeys and unto please what end?
Not to the glory of tyrant head but to

The being of body. Beauty is of body.
The flesh contouring shallowly on a head
Is a rock-garden needing body's love
And best bodiness to colorify

The big blue birds sitting and sea-shell flats
And caves, and on the iron acropolis
To spread the hyacinthine hair and rear
The olive garden for the nightingales.

Address to the Scholars
of New England

(*Harvard Phi Beta Kappa Poem, June 23, 1939*)

When Sarah Pierrepont let her spirit rage
Her love and scorn refused the bauble earth
(Which took bloom even here, under the Bear)
And groped for the Essence sitting in himself,
Subtle, I think, for a girl's unseasoned iago.

The late and sudden extravagance of soul
By which they all were swollen exalted her
At seventeen years to Edwards' canopy,
A match pleasing to any Heaven, had not
The twelve mortal labors harassed her soul.

Thrifty and too proud were the sea-borne fathers
Who fetched the Pure Idea in a bound box
And fastened him in a steeple, to have his court
Shabby with an unkingly establishment
And Sabbath levees for the minion fathers.

The majesty of Heaven has a great house,
And even if the Indian kingdom or the fox
Ran barking mad in a wide forest place,

93

They had his threshold, and you had the dream
Of property in him by a steepled house.

If once the entail shall come on raffish sons,
Knife-wit scholar and merchant sharp in thumb,
With positive steel they'll pry into the steeple,
And blinking through the cracked ribs at the void
A judgment laughter rakes the cynic sons.

But like prevailing wind New England's honor
Carried, and teased small Southern boys in school,
Whose heads the temperate birds fleeing your winter
Construed for, but the stiff heroes abashed
With their frozen fingers and unearthly honor.

Scared by the holy megrims of those Pilgrims,
I thought the unhumbled and outcast and cold
Were the rich Heirs traveling incognito,
Bred too fine for the country's sweet produce
And but affecting that dog's life of pilgrims.

There used to be debate of soul and body,
The soul storming incontinent with shrew's tongue
Against what natural brilliance body had loved,
Even the green phases though deciduous
Of earth's zodiac homage to the body.

Plato, before Plotinus gentled him,
Spoke the soul's part, and though its vice is known
We're in his shadow still, and it appears
Your founders most of all the nations held
By his scandal-mongering, and established him.

Perfect was the witch foundering in water,
The blasphemer that spraddled in the stocks,

94

The woman branded with her sin, the whales
Of ocean taken with a psalmer's sword,
The British tea infusing the bay's water.

But they reared heads into the always clouds
And stooped to the event of war or bread,
The secular perforces and short speech
Being labors surlily done with the left hand,
The chief strength giddying with transcendent clouds.

The tangent Heavens mocked the fathers' strength,
And how the young sons know it, and study now
To take fresh conquest of the conquered earth,
But they're too strong for that, you've seen them whip
The laggard will to deeds of lunatic strength.

To incline the powerful living unto peace
With Heaven is easier now, with Earth is hard,
Yet a rare metaphysic makes them one,
A gentle Majesty, whose myrtle and rain
Enforce the fathers' gravestones unto peace.

I saw the youngling bachelors of Harvard
Lit like torches, and scrambling to disperse
Like aimless firebrands pitiful to slake,
And if there's passion enough for half their flame,
Your wisdom has done this, sages of Harvard.

Master's in the Garden Again

(To the memory of Thomas Hardy)

i

Evening comes early, and soon discovers
Exchange between these conjugate lovers.

"Conrad! dear man, surprise! aren't you bold
To be sitting so late in your sodden garden?"

"Woman! intrusion! does this promise well?
I'm nursing my knees, they are not very cold.
Have you known the fall of the year when it fell?
Indeed it's a garden, but if you will pardon,
The health of a garden is reason's burden."

"Conrad! your feet are dripping in muck,
The neuralgia will settle in your own neck,
And whose health is it that catches an asthma?
Come in from foul weather for pity's sake!"

"No," says the thinker. "Concede. I am here,
Keeping guard of my garden and minding miasma.
You're lonely, my loony? Your house is up there.
Go and wait. If you won't, I'll go jump in the lake."

ii

And the master's back has not uncurved
Nor the autumn's blow for an instant swerved.

Autumn days in our section
Are the most used-up thing on earth
(Or in the waters under the earth)
Having no more color nor predilection
Than cornstalks too wet for the fire
And black leaves pitched onto the byre.

The show is of death. There is no defection.

iii

He will play out his mood before he takes food.

By the bob of the Power the dark skies lower,
By the bite of Its frost the children were lost
Who hurt no one where they shone in the sun,
But the valiant heart knows a better part
Than to do with an "O did It lay them low,
But we're a poor sinner just going to dinner."

See the tell-tale art of the champion heart.

Here's temple and brow, which frown like the law.
If the arm lies low, yet the rage looks high.
The accusing eye? that's a fierce round O.

The offense was raw, says the fix in the jaw.
We'll raise a rare row! we'll heave a brave blow!

A pantomime blow, if it damns him to do,
A yell mumming too. But it's gay garden now,
Play sweeter than pray, that the darkened be gay.

Prelude to an Evening

---

*(A poem revised and explicated: the soliloquy of a man
returning home to his wife)*

Do not enforce the tired wolf
Dragging his infected wound homeward
To sit tonight with the warm children
Saying the pretty Kings of France.

You are my scholar. Then languish, expire
With each day's terror and next week's doom
Till we're twice espoused, in love and ruin,
And grave but smiling though the heavens fall.

The images of the invaded mind
Were monstrous only in the dreams
Of your most brief enchanted headful.
Suppose a miracle of confusion:—

That dreamed and undreamt become each other
And mix the night and day of your soul.
For it never mattered your twice crying
From mouth unbeautied against the pillow

To avert the gun of the same old soldier,
If quickly cry, cock-crow or bell

Breaking the improbable black spell
Annihilated the poor phantom.

And now? To confirm our strange supposal,
Apparitions wait upon sunny mornings;
You in your peignoir commend the heaped oranges
Gold on the platter for cheeky children

But freeze at the turbulence under the floor
Where unclean spirits yawn and thrash;
The day-long clock will strike your fears;
The heels detonating the stair's cavern.

Freshening the water in the blue bowls
For the buckberries with not all your love
You listen for a low lost wind to awaken
The warning sibilance of pines.

Finally evening. Hear me denouncing
Our equal and conniving Furies;
You making Noes but they lack conviction;
Smoothing the heads of the hungry children.

I would have us magnificent at my coming;
Two souls tight-clasped; and a swamp of horrors.
O you shall be handsome and brave at fearing.
Now my step quickens; and meets a huge No!

Whose No was it? like the hoarse policeman's,
Clopping onstage in the Name of the Law.
That was Me; forbidding tricks at homecoming;
At the moment of coming to its white threshold.

I went to the nations of disorder
To be freed of the memory of good and evil;

There even your image was disfigured;
Then the boulevards rocked; they said, Go back.

I am here; and to balk my ruffian I bite
The tongue devising all that treason;
Then creep in my wounds to the sovereign flare
Of the room where you shine on the good children.

AND NOW FOR THE COMMENTARY. "Prelude to an Evening," in thirteen stanzas, is a new version of the original poem by that title, which had eight stanzas and was published thirty years ago. In the new poem the eight stanzas remain substantially about what they were before. If some of them have been tinkered with, that is according to the luxurious habit of poets, who, when an old poem comes up for republication, like to induce the whole delicious process of composition over again, and even try to make a few fresh beauties here and there if they can. The big change is the addition of four new stanzas at the end. They are like the others in form, being quatrains of unrhymed four-beat lines which mostly are end-stopped. It was my hope that the new stanzas would be like enough in tempo and style to keep continuity with the old ones as if by a single act of composition. But I am afraid that these so new and so few stanzas, doing so much in so short space, may be too brisk to suit with the others. What they must do is nothing less than undo the whole intention of the old poem, and bring it to a very different conclusion. Besides these four new stanzas there is another which makes a second stanza within the original eight. I wanted to define more sharply the situation which seemed to call for a reversal; now it takes nine stanzas, and has to be reversed in four.

Several friends have asked me to publish the reasons

why I thought I must change the ending so radically. The simple fact is that it became disagreeable to my ears as I continued to read it on public occasions now and then.

Here is a man returning in the evening from his worldly occupations to his own household. He has had plenty of encounters with the world's evils, and his imagination is immoderate and wayward; it has blown the evils up, till now he manages to be attended habitually by a vague but overwhelming impression of metaphysical Powers arrayed against him; he can say even to others (if they are capable of sympathy) that he is a man pursued by Furies. And he cannot but think it an anticlimax, a defeat unworthy of his confrontation of his fate, to spend the evening with children at their lessons. The poem is the man's soliloquy as he approaches his house. He is addressing the mother of his children, who awaits him, as if rehearsing the speech he will make in her presence in order to persuade her to share his fearful preoccupations and give him her entire allegiance. He seems to think he will win her over; there is no intimation that it may turn out quite differently. But suppose he succeeds: will not that be a dreary fate for the woman? And what of the children? Those are not his questions. But they came to be mine. By the end of the ninth stanza he pictures her prophetically as rapt in her new terrors, almost to the point of forgetting the children; if they are hungry, she will absent-mindedly smooth their heads.

I suppose a poet is excused without having to invoke the Fifth Amendment if he believes in his own poem, at least at the stage of first publication. My liking went quite beyond its merits, and lasted much too long. It had to do with some notion of a workmanlike poetic line carrying forward the argument while the woman was being borne through successive terrors not of her own making, yet still invested in her incorruptible dignity. It was with intense pleasure that I watched her suffering there; she was a heroine almost after the pattern of some diminutive classical tragedy. And if the piece had a hero, it must be the husband and speaker. I had not come to saying that the man was odious, that he was, incontestably, the villain. That was rather strange. As for my ordinary conscience in these matters, I believe I have only one other poem so vindictive as this, and I know some readers to whom it is no secret which it must be. It is the one called "Blue Girls," where the girls in the schoolyard are preening themselves in their beauty (as they should) till a man looking on addresses them and forces them to take account of a blear-eyed old woman whom he invents on the spot, and describes, with the threat that to her favor they must come soon.

At any rate. One day last winter, what I had not said was said for me; by a strong-minded young woman writing in a very little magazine devoted to the "explication" of difficult verse, in answer to a subscriber's query. What did the man of my poem mean to do? She replied with a commendable severity: this man was simply a brutal character who meant not to do any baby-sitting even if the babies were his own. At once I conceded the justice of her observation, and with more relief than surprise. All the same, I was soon wondering if I might not somehow patch up the poem and save it; by saving the woman and the children from their distress; and of course by saving the villain too, who so far as the genders go belonged to my party. I rather thought not. If I must administer to him a speedy and radical "conversion" after many stanzas of villainy— the idea was too forbidding.

But another event brought me back to my project of salvage. Six years ago Charles Coffin, my teaching colleague, died at the Huntington Library in the midst of his studies of the theology of *Paradise Lost*. Now Milton

103

had notoriously been a sort of independent theologian; but I was aware that Dr. Coffin, for all his churchmanship, inclined to be an independent theologian too. Unfortunately his packed notebooks were far from complete. But a faithful pupil rescued one complete section or chapter under the title of "Creation and the Self," which he submitted to *ELH* (*A Journal of English Literary History*); it was published in March 1962. The essay might have been the key chapter of the book. It deals first with the magnanimous creation of man in the Creator's image, and then with the man's adventurous behaviors as they affected his relations with the Creator. We must remember that the writer was exploring the mind of Milton, and limiting his speculation scrupulously to the theological ideas that were feasible at the date of Milton's poem. Milton's theme, said Dr. Coffin, is the story of the friendly association between Creator and creature; it is broken many times by the creature's misdeameanors, but the Creator always is prepared to extend his grace; may I remark, though it will be something of an anachronism: as if He had allowed for them in advance? If the creature repents, the happy connection is restored.

I have liked this theology so much for its friendly note that now, and from here on, I will refer symbolically to the man in my poem as Adam, and to the woman whom he apostrophizes as Eve; these are the names they must bear in our Great Myth. In this way I shall not be altogether compromising my poem by "explicating" it. A poem is not a moral essay nor a religious tract; it is best if our talk about it falls short of being just that. We are still feeling the scars of a long, confused period in the modern history of literary criticism in which this issue has been fought over, and perhaps fought out. Poetry is still the supremely inclusive speech which escapes, as if unaware of them, the strictures and reductions of the systematic logical understanding. Publicly or tacitly, we probably all have some sort of theology, and its teachings are quite capable of entering into a poem, perhaps without losing any of their compulsion. It is difficult to write the proper poem nowadays, because after many ages of hard prose we have come far from the primitive and natural speech of poetry. But it is still being handsomely done. In a true poem it is as if the religious dogma or the moral maxim had been dropped into the pot as soon as the act of composition began; sinking down out of sight and consciousness, it is as if it became a fluid and was transfused into the bloodstream of the poet now, and would be communicated to the bloodstream of his auditors eventually. The significance of the poem is received by feeling; or, more technically, by immediate unconscious intuition. So let the man of my poem be Adam, let the woman and mother of his children be Eve; if the poem did not name them, let the commentary do it. At once we are moving over an old and familiar terrain; bearing these names the figures will be invested for everybody with their moral and religious properties.

I cannot fail to remark that I was partly prepared for this symbolic sense of my characters by an event dated 1961: the publication of *The Rhetoric of Religion* by Kenneth Burke; a book which for the largeness of its perspective and the scruple of its discriminations must rate among the important treatises of philosophy. In his foreword Burke remarks:

> The subject of religion falls under the head of *rhetoric* in the sense that rhetoric is the art of *persuasion*, and religious cosmogonies are designed . . . as exceptionally thoroughgoing modes of persuasion. To persuade men towards certain acts, religions would form the kinds of attitude which prepare men for

such acts. And in order to plead for such attitudes as persuasively as possible, the religious always ground their exhortations (to themselves and others) in statements of the widest and deepest possible scope, concerning the authorship of men's motives.

A less hortatory form of persuasion, yet a powerful and rhetorical one, is poetry; and it has to be said that Burke as a cunning verbalist has an extraordinary sensibility for the varied meanings that go with a word or phrase. And Burke would think, as I do, that it is more faithful to the sense of a serious poem to translate it into theology, if we must translate it, than into morality. A poem starts with a crucial human situation, and from there proceeds usually by some mixture of drama, narrative, and contemplation. But does not the priest himself teach theology to the congregation most effectively by means of Scriptural narratives and ritualistic drama? The secular-seeming ordinary poem plies its rhetoric through common words, but theology pervades them invisibly. So digressive, and regressive, is the significance of old words even though we may not choose to stop and dwell on them.

But Charles Coffin supplied my most immediate cues. Adam, he said, was the noblest of God's creatures because he was created free; he could choose his own actions. But to guide him he had reason, which was akin to his Creator's; and imagination, so that he might be in his degree a creator in his own right. Imagination is a great term in the Scriptures, but I am afraid that its usual employment there is by way of mention of the evil imaginations of the heart. How prodigious are Adam's creations, even since Milton's time; especially since Milton's time. He has created commodities exactly suited to his physical need, and machines too, to which he has delegated their automatic creation; and terrible engines of war; and as I think we all think increasingly, a foolish clutter of little machines and mechanisms which by saving his strength impoverish it, leaving his body soft and his mind aimless as to its proper objects. He has created gods in his own image, but sometimes they are not flattering to his intelligence, and not fit for universal worship. Finally, there are his poems, and other works of art, sometimes famed everywhere and regarded as all but everlasting monuments; and they might always have been beneficent and tonic, but often are only hateful. The fictitious Adam of my eight stanzas has a speech precisely as pretty as his zealous author and patron could find for him, but the ruling imagination is that of a "wicked heart"; for this I regret to think that the real Adam his maker is responsible also.

Had we not better say that Adam was created half free, not wholly free? A theme which is not particularly explored in Scripture, but doubtless is there gratefully taken for granted, is that of the marvelous body created to house Adam's soul; replenishing, conditioning, repairing, preserving itself, almost without Adam's consciousness; a machine not of Adam's manufacture, but the fortress and security of his free enterprise. A tight and physical containment is appointed to the body; much of Adam's vital strength must be expended upon its secret operation, and it is just as well if it has not the freedom of Adam's imagination.

We come to Charles Coffin's account of Eve, and here I am all eyes and ears. ("Now my step quickens," says the Adam of my poem.) It appears that the agency in Eve's creation was Adam's as well as the Creator's. Adam took the initiative; he asked for it. Therefore it was from his body that the Creator got the rib out of which she was to be fashioned. This is not to say that the new creature was not as fully authorized as Adam. But she was a more separate and independent creature, says Dr. Coffin. God talks familiarly with Adam but not with Eve. Raphael talks at great length with Adam, but Eve after serving dinner stays discreetly in the background; and when he takes up the "abstruse" matter of the motions of the celestial universe she steals away to her flowers. Adam will explain all this to her later if she wishes. Clearly there is a deficiency in Eve's composition as compared with Adam's. She is not of the "intellectual" type, and it does not seem likely that she will be in all respects his congenial companion; there may have been some irony in the Creator's mind in complying with Adam's request.

Eve is freer than Adam in some respects, and is so declared by Dr. Coffin; she is more natural, confirmed in her direction already, therefore more spontaneous in her responses; she is less reflective. Her deficiency is in the freedom of those adventurous behaviors which go with rational discourse and the metaphysical imagination. So far as my eight stanzas are concerned, the matter turns on whether she is free to respond to the interests of her spouse as an artist; whose art this time is an extravagant "supposal" or fantasy, having a theological cast and an evil imagination. Is she capable of being swept off her feet by a work of art—especially one that invokes a vision of evil? Adam hopes to find her capable. But the answer is in the new stanzas. He concedes that she is not capable; he will not ask of her the impossible. She is less free than Adam. Speaking very roughly, let us say that she is one-quarter free.

I found these considerations somewhat chilling. But I asked myself: what development within Eve's personality was so uniquely important that it must replace the missing quarter of her freedom? The answer was not really difficult, and it could be checked against Scripture and Milton rather explicitly. Eve has a special function within her body, and for exercising it a virtue, a habit not acquired but already built into her unconscious mind. Behind it a quarter of her vital energy (if we have to quantify it) has been committed firmly to its consummation. She bears the children in her own body; then she cares for them, teaches them, defends them to the last extremity, even with her life if necessary. One of the most vivid of my memories comes back whenever I think of Eve's composition. It is the recollection of my first "tutorial" in my Oxford college. When I had read my appointed paper, there came the instant suggestion, from the formidable philosopher who was my tutor, that I possess myself at once of *The Origin and Development of the Moral Ideas*, in two large volumes, published in 1906, by Edward Westermarck, professor of moral philosophy at the University of Finland, professor of sociology at the University of London. Two days later I was reading the chapter in which the "maternal instinct" is described as the origin of all human altruism. For the moral ideas of the male have to do with such motives as power, prestige, and aggressiveness. At once I reflected that no altruism is needed to motivate the conception of offspring; that is so important for family and tribe and history that in the scheme of creation the act was invested for both parties with a bodily pleasure so massive that it must prove more than ample for its occasions. The rearing of the children does not have such a sure sanction; unless it is the sanction of Eve's natural goodness, of the tender mercies which are sealed within her, awaiting with confidence their occasions.

This paragraph will carry a slightly rueful self-appraisal. Probably the most of my poems are about familiar and familial situations; domestic and homely things. Eventually I was surprised and rather set back by the sense of what a "bourgeois" poet they had turned me into. The "Prelude" seemed to promise a variation in my performance, but even here it is evident that I have reverted. The change of tune in the four new stanzas, and the abject capitulation of Adam, may cause me to be drummed out of the corps of smart and reputable poets; for surely within the whole circuit of poetic occasions I have descended to the nadir of available themes in order to occupy myself with—a baby-sitting. My pedestrian and precarious defense could only be the argument that in the degree of their commonplace such situations might be denoting precisely those patterns within the great Familial Configuration which had been ordained in our creation, and were therefore the ones likely to be standard and permanent.

Will my readers speculate and generalize with me a little? Suppose Eve first tempted Adam, whether or not instructed by a kindly Serpent as to the facts of life; for she would need to have a prescience of the sequel. She was successful; and perhaps she despised Adam a little for the innocence and haste with which he yielded. Then came the children. After this it would be Adam soliciting Eve; but if possible it would be on his own lordly conditions. Let her share his professional interests; then she will have his preoccupations, sometimes as evil as they will be good, but she will also have him; he may even suggest that less time should be spent with the children. But, even before Adam comes into her presence to make his proposition, he is condemned out of his own mouth. The children must occupy her mind now; they have replaced their father in her deepest affections; and if he desires her favors he will have to take them not on his terms but on hers, which will stipulate that he must share the responsibility for the children. I am aware that both Israel (which was responsible for the Old Testament) and Milton (who elaborated on its story) took a partisan view of Adam as the lord of the household. There has been much question of Milton's personal success in this role. But it was within the history of Israel, from the beginning to this day, that

110

I could easily imagine that Adam's talent for the familial role had been altogether exceptional.

The tenth stanza continues the ninth, by providing a passage with erotic connotations, in order to display Adam truthfully; that requires its first three lines. The fourth line begins the denouement. Suddenly, as Adam approaches, he comes to his senses and knows that Eve will never accept his invitation; not the open and intellectual part, not the implicit erotic part if that is bound up with the other. He knows better than to say it to her actual person. Probably he will never say it out loud.

The twelfth stanza recalls a truancy of Adam's at some time or other, when he had gone among strangers trying to forget his Eve, whose feelings for him had not been the same after the coming of the children. He went on a journey. But what he found was that Eve was still the only woman for him. We respect his constancy.

In the last stanza Adam stands on the threshold of his house, but he stops a moment to fortify his wiser self against his own self-defeating eloquence. The final utterance of his soliloquy, and of the poem, is a two-line homage, half mystical, perhaps half maudlin, to the formidable yet beneficent dignity of her status and that of the children. We imagine that he is going to enjoy her favor, but his immediate motive is under the familial sign. He will sit with the children dutifully and, we will think, proudly. It is not the happiest ending that he could possibly conceive, but it is the best he had the right to expect. Perhaps a kindly reader will wish him many happy returns of his homecoming. Does not the poem presuppose a crucial and habit-forming moment in his history? There will be many interims yet when he will be out in the free world again, busied in his own way professionally. But every time he takes his leave he will have said to them and himself: I shall return.

A Note on the Type

THIS BOOK is set in ELECTRA, a Linotype face designed by W. A. Dwiggins (1880–1956). This face cannot be classified as either modern or old-style. It is not based on any historical model, nor does it echo any particular period or style. It avoids the extreme contrasts between thick and thin elements that mark most modern faces, and attempts to give a feeling of fluidity, power, and speed.

Composed, printed, and bound by
Kingsport Press, Inc., Kingsport, Tennessee.
Binding based on an original design
by W. A. Dwiggins.
Typography by Vincent Torre

A Note about the Author

JOHN CROWE RANSOM was born in Pulaski, Tennessee, in 1888. After attending Vanderbilt and Oxford (as a Rhodes Scholar), he was a member of the faculty of Vanderbilt University from 1914 to 1937. He then taught at Kenyon College for twenty years and edited the *Kenyon Review*, from its founding in 1939. He has had published more than a dozen volumes of poetry and criticism, and has received the Bollingen Prize for Poetry, the Russell Loines Memorial Fund Prize, and the 1962 Fellowship Prize of the Academy of American Poets. Mr. Ransom lives in Gambier, Ohio, having retired from teaching five years ago, and is working on some new poetry

May 1963